RESILIENCE THROUGH THE EYES OF MY READERS

DAMAN DEV SOOD, FBCI, FBCS, CBCI

IEEE Ambassador

Member Champion – IEEE India MOVE, Partner Relations Committee

IEEE Computer Society Distinguished Contributor, (Inaugural Class)

Chair – Public Relations & Publication Standing Committee, IEEE Delhi Section

Toastmaster

BCI's C&R Business Continuity Manager of the Year Award India 2009

BCI's Merit Award Global 2012

BCI's Continuity & Resilience Contributor Award Middle East 2020 (and Global Finalist)

DRII's Lifetime Achievement Award 2021(Finalist)

BCI's Continuity & Resilience Contributor Award Global, India & South Asia 2021

BCI's Hall of Fame

ILA's Global Outstanding Leadership Award 2021

DRII's Lifetime Achievement Award 2022(Finalist)

Qualified Independent Director

(Ministry of Corporate Affairs, Govt. of India scheme)

Certified International Trainer, Certified Corporate Trainer

International Resilience Trainer & Consultant|| 10000+ hours Training/ Teaching|| Speaker|| Author|| BCM|| Risk Management|| Crisis Management||

Organisational Resilience|| Operational Resilience|| Cybersecurity||

Qualified Independent Director|| Mentor|| Toastmaster

To My Readers: With Best Wishes!

This is a special creation for our son Divij on his 29th birthday!

And to the rest of my family (My Resilience journey would not be complete and successful without their support). Special thanks to my wife Bhavna – who has always been a great support.

I owe thanks to Anchita Sood for editing the book, and to Tanuj Sood for designing the cover pages.

The book is a compilation of reviews by my readers for two of my books:

1. My Experiments with BCM and

2. My Experiments with Organisational Resilience: Part I

I have not taken their consent specifically, but they had agreed for me to use their feedback/ reviews/ comments in promoting my books. Some of those reviews were very detailed ones and presented their own understanding of my writings. Hence, I was inclined to publish this compilation – I have included all references.

This book will not be complete without my readers – so additional thanks to them.

Contents

Chapter 1: The Best That A Son Could Have Said About A Father

Divij had written this review of my first book 'My Experiments with BCM'. I got it colour printed and framed and is in our room – I see it many times a day. This is my best inspiration since then – I have read it many times and this keeps me reminding to do more and to do better.

This is how the idea was generated to compile all reviews in the form of a book. And the book had to open with this chapter although I have had forewords and reviews by many more senior professionals.

Here it goes…

Divij Sood, Gameplay Engineer at Improbable, UK| ✏ Co-founder at DyonisianWriting - Results-focused Content Marketing

As a son, you don't often understand what your dad does very well.

While growing up, when my dad was a "Computer Consultant" at TCS, I remember wondering if his whole job was printing out fliers and recruiting more consultants!

But one part of dad's career as a "Global BCM and Resilience Practitioner", CIO, COO, and everything else he's been in the last few years, that specifically stood out to me, was the very real recognition he got as a "Global Leader". He was winning multiple awards every year.

And even though I didn't understand exactly what he did and how well he did it, I was in awe and admiration for all the awards and recognition he got for his work both inside and outside the office.

So here it is - the book that's finally helped me understand what exactly he's been doing all these years!

There are tons of lessons here from throughout his life that anyone aspiring to be a BCM professional can learn from.

But there are also a lot of lessons that anyone, regardless of career, can learn from. Even me.

Most of these lessons are very recent and relevant too - including how COVID is a disaster that needs the application of "BCM" in everyday life. So what better way to learn than from a BCM world leader?

Plus, there's a hidden gem - the longest and most detailed chapter in here - explains everything I wanted to know about how he aims for and wins all those professional recognition awards. 100% applicable to anyone regardless of profession.

All the other chapters are concise and easy to follow - often just a single page long.

So don't put it off - grab your own copy and read through the life of Global Leader in BCM, Daman Dev Sood, in 100 concise and quick chapters.

Section 1: Based on 'My Experiments with BCM'

1.1 Andrew Hiles

Founder, BCI, Professor Emeritus of BCM at Telfort Business Institute, Shanghai University.

Anything Daman Dev Sood writes is worth reading. If you buy a BCM book in 2022, make it this one.

Well done, Daman Dev Sood. I hope you break all records for sales of a BCM/ resilience book.

1.2 Anil Kumar Chawla

Building a culture of business continuity

Reviewed in India on 10 January 2022

Daman's book is an easy flowing reading. Starting with his own life since childhood, he builds the narr to BCM gradually. Incidents leading to learning which stays for life, anecdotes, experiences from work non-work life sustain the reader's interest. One does not realize when he/she learnt the essence of BC deliberately or inadvertently.
Must read for all those who are in the field.

1.3 Alex Fulick

MBCI, CBCP, CBRA, aBCF, CORS – Creator and Host of Preparing for the Unexpected, author of 'Planning and Performing the Business Impact Assessment.'

There are lots of great stories and personal anecdotes. Daman certainly identifies lots of relatable challenges that many BCM professionals experience, regardless of their industry or location."

1.4 JB Koul

Amazon Customer

★★★★★ **Very good read for BCM practioners**

Reviewed in India on 4 January 2022

Verified Purchase

Review for Daman's book," My experiments with BCM"
Daman has shared some of the experiences from his BCM journey in a very easy to read manner. These stories or anecdotes resonate closely with me as I've had similar experiences in my BCM journey. Many of us, working in the BCM world, have faced similar issues, challenges and have responded in different ways with different outcomes. Daman has highlighted a very important point for BCM practitioners – we need t "blow our own trumpet" which means we need to keep highlighting the impact we make to business. Today BCM is not just a "minimum compliance requirement "but a "differentiator to business" and I would say Daman has played a key role in highlighting this key point.

J.B.Koul
Experienced BCM professional

1.5 Marcela Calero

Experienced Professional in Project Management, Operations, Business Continuity, Business Development and Change Management PM, LSSGBPC, SFC, ISO22301

I have thoroughly enjoyed reading Daman's book. The language he has used to narrate his experiences in life and BCM is one that is easy to follow, relates to and of utmost value. From his childhood experiences, the respect to his elders, the contribution to others and his ability to adapt to situations and learn, and teach, and keep on that virtuous cycle of living, learning, teaching, experimenting and leading, makes it a worth reading.

1.6 An Amazon Customer

 PG

★★★★★ **Great Book for people who want to understand Business Continuity Management**

Reviewed in India on 10 December 2021

Verified Purchase

Daman is a global leader in BCM. This book was recommended to our organization. It was one of the best recommendations.

Daman makes the tough topic of BCM very interesting. The personal touch of the book makes BCM study like a biography, which makes this book stand out among other books.

Highly recommended for people

1. Professionals who wants to know more BCM.
2. Leaders who want to see practical problems and solutions
3. Students who want to learn about BCM
4. Curious readers who want to diversify their knowledge

1.7 Phillip Igmedio Cruz

Phillip Igmedio Cruz is Sr. Business Continuity Head for ING Business Shared Services. Formerly: Global BCM Head for Lufthansa Global Business Services; Country BCM Head for Accenture Philippines Business Process Outsourcing; Country IT Head for Ford Motor Company Philippines

Very interesting read about a person who is an expert in the field and has not only gone through a lot but is also a recognized expert. I really liked learning the nitty-gritties in Section 28 – "How to win BCI awards”.

1.8 Praveen Jain

Praveen Jain

January 10 at 11:08 PM ·

Review of Book on Amazon : "My experiments with BCM By Daman Sood"

"My Experiments with BCM" is an excellent must read book for all those who are pursuing a career in Business Continuity Management worldwide. Daman is a global BCM mentor and has candidly shared and correlated his own experiences and learnings during his BCM journey over the last 16 years. The book is a valuable collection of curious & inquisitive approach of his identifying risks and threats, their likely Business Impacts with possible required actions and their timely mitigation solutions. It is my conviction that BCM Professionals globally and across their business lines will immensely benefit with various narrations in the book and get a novel and deeper insight with a different perspective and dimension to various BCM encounters.

The book will be a success ladder for all BCM professionals internationally.

'Recommended collection in all personal / official libraries.'

Book Link on Amazon:
My Experiments with BCM: My BCM journey = Your BCM mentor/companion

1.9 Elvin Chan

MBCP FBCI JD CPA CISA CEng | Director, Head of Asia Pacific Business Continuity Management | Royal Bank of Canada

Reading through the chapters is like chatting with an old friend by the fireside, listening to all short stories about the life of one of the most seasoned BCM practitioners in the region. Such life experiences or even tricks you won't be able to learn from any traditional textbooks. If you are a BCM practitioner, you would smile when you go through some of the stories as you were definitely in a similar situation before too. It's one of the most refreshing and interesting reads for me for a long time. Brilliant!

1.10 Rishi Kumar

Rishi Kumar • 1st
AVP | Digital Transformation| Enterprise Agility| Global Client Partnerships | Pr...
3w •

Recently read an excellent book from our own **Daman Dev Sood**. Congratulations on your book. It allowed me to learn more about you than I already know based on our long association. It is definitely a good read for everyone to learn from your knowledge and experiences. I loved all other learnings chapters as well!

1.11 Manish Walia

Senior Organizational Resilience and Cyber Defense Professional

My Experiments with BCM is a candid expression of Daman's journey as a person as well as a professional. Anyone who knows Daman can vouch for his unparalleled commitment to integrity and that does reflect in this body of work as well. I thoroughly enjoyed reading this book and would recommend it to anyone in need of some inspiration.

1.12 Nitin Vaidya

Nitin Vaidya

A holistic view in BCM

Reviewed in India on 14 January 2022

I read and continued reading. Reason - Business Continuity is so near to my heart. Being a Business Continuity practitioner myself, I emphasize everyone that BCM is not about BC of a 30Bn+ company. It about each and everything around us, in our family, in every company, every business... just everywher See the section 'My worst Case'. This book presents the journey that makes a Mind - A Business Contin Practitioner. The books has so many points that will make you reflect and help develop you as a compl BCM practitioner. Great Reading.... Daman - keep sharing!!!

1.13 Andy Osborne

Consultant, trainer and author (Practical Business Continuity Management and Risk Management Simplified).

The style, of part-autobiography, part how-to, is quite different to most BCM books and I like stories that relate BCM to 'normal' real-life experiences. I'm sure people 'in the business', like me, will be interested to know Daman's story of his life in, and thoughts on, BCM .

1.14 S Walia

S Walia

★★★★★ **A must read for all BCM and Operational Resilience professionals.**

Reviewed in India on 13 January 2022

A well written and yet extensive book on a continually evolving subject. My experiments with BCM is truthfully intriguing, so much so that while going through the chapters of this book, you can correlate your own life and work experiences to those in the book and that gives you insights to what you as a BCM Porfessional could have done differently. I strongly recommend this body of work to all BCM / Operational Resilience professionals as it can truly change the way we look at the subject.

1.15 Mark J Carroll

SVP – Business Risk Officer, Income Research + Management

There's an old fable about a young boy who wants to build up his arm muscles so he approaches the local town wise man, a gentlemen who lays all day in his hammock, just contemplating. The boy asks him for his insight and the wise man tells the boy that he will 'work on it' but that the boy needs to chop some wood as payment for the man's 'services'. After days of wood chopping the frustrated boy confronts the wise man for his answer. The wise man tells the boy to make a muscle and to his surprise, his arms are built up.

Apologies for the long lead in, but that is how I think about Daman's book. The reading is interesting and entertaining as ideas and thoughts become inculcated into your mindset without you even knowing it, like the learnings we get from a fable which is actually real.

I can personally identify with much of this as I evolved as a COBOL programmer to a BCM educator and practitioner and have met and worked with many of those in his stories as well as having experienced the infamous far east cable cut, Y2K, etc. But aside from my personal connection, there is something in this work for everybody.

1.16 Shrey Jain

Shrey Jain • 1st
Deputy Engineer at Bharat Electronics Ltd.
18h •

The book "My Experiments with BCM" is an excellent reference for Business Continuity Management professionals globally.

Daman Dev Sood 'Resilient People - Resilient Planet' sir is among one of the proficient global BCM trainers, mentors and guide and has honestly shared his BCM challenges, learnings and experiences of last 16 years applicable across the Industry.

The book is a cherished collection of interesting stories and has a unique way of recognizing BCM challenges, probable risks and threats and their likely impacts on Business. The learnings from the book will surely help in advance and timely actions to overcome Business challenges with possible solutions.

The stories in the book give a new dimension to the thinking process to find timely and valuable solutions to likely BCM challenges that may possibly be survival threat in future.

1.17 Anand Singh Chandel

SVP, Team Head HRIS Adoption & Innovations, DBS Bank Singapore

I have known Daman for many years, from being a junior to him in our polytechnic days to working together in TCS including spending sometime with same client in Edinburgh to many nights in the data center where he trained and guided me in very initial days. After a few years, we both went our ways to different parts of the world on our own journeys, meeting online and offline intermittently. But one thing that I have always known is his passion for his work and truth which also comes out in his book here.

He does come out unconventional a lot, but looking a bit deeper there is always a lot of conventional wisdom in his words. The same is very apparent in his book - which he has communicated beautifully as something you will converse with close friends over a cup of tea - with snippets of life and career and experience and knowledge. Each chapter nuggets of advise and learnings - both on personal development but most importantly on BCM practices. Each client interaction has details which BCM and IT practitioners are always aware of - but presented in a wonderful contextual way which can be used to justify any business case.

And then in chapter 73 - bringing the practice to home is just wonderful, an aspect which we all miss out.

Kudos to Daman for a well written book about his life and BCM practice.

1.18 Arunkumar. B

Book Review of "My Experiments with BCM: My BCM journey" by Shri.Daman Dev Sood

Reviewed in India on 30 January 2022

The book was an interesting read. I could finish the entire book in one go and could not take my eyes off it! The flow was lucid, interesting and thoughtful, filled with the author's rich professional experience, anecdotes and most importantly, checklists. The author also touches upon key aspects like being an example and leading from the front when the odds are down. Chapters with anecdotes on dealing with different cultures, top management, respecting elders, (a personal) CSR initiative to impart knowledge to the "have nots" were all impressive. The crowning jewel to me was Chapter #16, Bullet #5 "Blow your trumpet" where he has brought out a key to success, quoting him verbatim "make noise about each step – application submitted/we are participating/have been shortlisted/are winner or runner up etc. Run a test, manage an incident, be transparent and share the report of all of these with all the employees". Definitely a book from an experienced professional worth owning/reading! Thanks and Kudos to the Author for bringing out such a wonderful book! Keep it up Daman Saab!

1.19 Radha Vijayaraghavan

CEO- REV Consulting

"Daman's book is a reader's delight on a difficult to comprehend subject.

It has been a great learning experience to go through the real-life examples quoted under apt chapter headings.

Daman's inspiring and resilient personality shines through the BCM story that he has 'Designed, Developed and Delivered' with telling effect."

Wishing you all the Best on your next book!!

1.20 Gourav

Gourav

Interesting Read

Reviewed in India on 31 January 2022

I have known the author for quite a longtime and this book has indeed come out as a reference point to understand why and how someone of this level of experienc and journey behaves in a particular way. It is a good read for those starting their careers and professional journey in any field. All the best for the next one. Cheers.

Thank you for your feedback. | Report abuse

1.21 Akshay Bhargava

Head – Business Operations, Education BU,

Tata Consultancy Services

Simply a WOW. Its simply awesome. No words to describe it. Though the topic is BCM and most discussions are around BC, the way each point and story have been narrated is very captivating.

I could not stop myself until I completed it just now. The way you have written this book, as Elvin from Hong Kong has mentioned, its just like chatting with you. So easy to read, comprehend and understand the seriousness of BC through the example stories.

1.22 Joop Frankle

Certified BC Professional

Amazon Customer

Start reading and you can't stop

Beoordeeld in Nederland op 21 januari 2022

Daman Dev Sood 'Resilient People - Resilient Planet' "My experiments with "truth" BCM"

Thank you Daman for taking me with you on a journey with your experiments with BCM. It was a pleasure to read your book and on the way sometimes I recognized myself.

Read his book and take your journey with Daman as your guide and use his information, ideas and examples to help you implementing BCM in your organization.

Chapter 83 brings a smile on my face. That's what we do!

I needed only a few hours to fulfil my journey that's because the book is so easy to read and he is so passionate as I am with BCM. And it is not only the passion for BCM he has but also a passion to help and teach other people voluntary with the same passion.

Once you start reading you won't stop anymore.

1.23 Bal Mukund Jha

B.Tech (E&T), M.Tech, MBA(HR), Certified PMP, ISO 45001 Lead Auditor and Trainer

The title of the book itself sets the tone of interest for the reader. The chapters beautifully elaborate this very title of "My Experiments…..". Almost every nook and cranny of BCM Concepts in corporate world has been presented by Mr. Daman. And not only the corporate world, but this book has been successful in extending its scope in one's personal life as well.

The innovative idea of "Daman's Thermometer" has been presented with brilliance. I can safely declare that this book is a wonderful journey for a BCM practitioner. As a reader, it never tested my resilience because reading such material was equivalent to smooth handholding by a mentor. Reading the book gave a spell bound experience.

My best wishes to Daman Ji for his next book on Organizational Resilience.

1.24 Sanketa Anand

EdTech Business Evangelist and Entrepreneur

This book covers very key areas of BCP, given the uncertainty around us. Coming from Daman, makes it lot more practical given his wide experience in the Industry. Some of the incidents and relevant stories narrated in the book are very relevant for dynamic organizations and world.

As I see, this book will open many eyes right from organizations to individuals who in their own personal life need to have a continuity.

Great Read. Highly recommended.

Section 2: Based on 'My Experiments with Organisational Resilience: Part I'

2.1 Andrew Hiles

Founder, BCI, Professor Emeritus of BCM at Telfort Business Institute, Shanghai University.

When I read Daman Dev Sood's last book, recommended it as the 2022 must buy book for BCM & resilience professionals.

I thought it would be a difficult, if not an impossible, act to follow.

It takes a lot of hard work to make something look as easy as this, his latest book.

Creating a work that is at the same time scholarly, highly readable and compassionate is no mean feat, it is the unicorn of writing.

But the author has succeeded brilliantly in delivering such a book.

Have known Daman for over 30 years as a respected competitor, colleague, and friend.

He constantly surprises me with more practical, actionable insights into the legitimate scope of continuity and resilience.

Each year I read of deaths of those who helped me launch business continuity and moved it forward to become a recognised profession.

Christmas 2022 is fast approaching as I write this foreword.

It is a time of reflection.

A time to remember and give thanks to those who helped me and BCM on our journeys.

It is a time to look forward to the future of the profession a dozen of us BCM pioneers created.

That future is in safe hands.

Input from round the world identifies at least a dozen resilience and BCM practitioners that are the equals, if not the betters, of those pioneers.

I am proud to have been asked to write this foreword for one of them.

2.2 JB Koul

Resilience Practitioner

Just finished reading the book "My Experiments with Organisational Resilience Part 1", written by Daman Dev Sood.

My first impressions on this book:

This book provides a very good overview on Organisational Resilience to anybody who is trying to understand what Organisational Resilience is all about.

The "snippet" style in which different aspects are shared in the book make it both easy to read as well as interesting.

BCM and Resilience are not the same thing and Resilience is the logical next step in the natural evolution of Business Continuity Management. It is the need for every function and every person in the organisation to work towards this goal.

Another important aspect is the focus on people - if people are resilient, organisations will be resilient. Just like BCM is the job of every employee in an organisation, so is Resilience, the responsibility of everyone in an organisation.

Daman has used references from McKinsey and Harvard to reinforce the less understood and less talked aspects of Organisational Resilience regarding Human Resource Management, environment, communications and Supply Chain Management.

This book is an excellent read for all professionals who are looking for the answers to the question - What is the next step in the evolution of BCM and where do we go from here?

2.3 Akshay Bhargava

India - Head – Business Operations, Education BU,

Tata Consultancy Services

This is simply a WOW !!!!!!!!!!!!!!!!!!!!!! This book is just too good and captivating.

Starting with Aunty's story connects at an emotional level and though of course full of anxiety, does tend to lead the readers and conveys the message clearly.

The simple language used throughout with the short stories and thought-provoking ideas is simply amazing. I am personally able to relate this with the various aspects we encounter in office on a regular basis – like focusing on weaknesses rather than building on strengths. It's like the story where a school was opened in the jungle and at the end an exam was taken and the monkey flopped in swimming, whereas the fish could not climb trees, ignoring the strengths of each animal.

We often find the leadership lacking, but you have aptly conveyed the message that it starts from us – we always expect it to start somewhere else. Your examples from your own life (like the boy who was punished since you said he had eaten from the bin) apart from sending the messages also convey that we are not the only ones who have committed mistakes (maybe blunders) in life. If such distinguished people like yourself could have done some mistakes in life, a message which does go out is that this is human as long as we ponder over it and try to correct it (or a similar situation) in future.

Another point often talked about, which is unlike what is practiced across the globe these days is the respect we should have for one another irrespective of the differences on beliefs, genders, religion, elder / younger, etc. Somehow though we talk about it, the fact is, it seems to be somehow getting diluted in the race for growth, which unfortunately is limited to financials and business without emphasising on the respect part, though as you have rightly mentioned, if we can practice it, we can expect better results.

Overall, I felt that the messages being conveyed, though common sensical (and simplification) are missing in our lives and this book is a reminder for bringing them back in life. The embedded graphs and pictures helped a lot in understanding the concept with fewer words and with a better impact.

Wish you all the very best for this book and the others expected in future too. Thanks a lot for sharing this copy with me. It was indeed a pleasure reading it and just like Phillip, I guess I will also be reading this at least a few times to get the crux in detail.

2.4 Rajesh Vaish

Formerly with Global IT Centre of State Bank of India

DFS, Ministry of Finance, Government of India

We have all experimented with Business Continuity Management, Risk Management, Disaster Management, Disaster Recovery, Cyber Security… but few have explored Organisational Resilience (ISO 22316: 2017). It is interesting to see Daman Dev Sood's "MY EXPERIMENTS WITH ORGANISATIONAL RESILIENCE".

What apt definition of a Resilient Organisation: a risk managing, learning and continually improving Organisation.

Organisational Resilience is a journey of transformation, continual change, incessant innovation; a focus on resolute purpose, shared values and common culture; a commitment to integrity, diversity, equity and inclusion.

A Resilient Organisation takes care of the triple bottom line (people, profit, planet) and makes it sustainable. To be resilient, the author's prescription is: think, think creatively, think out of the box; do different; create a culture of listening and speaking up; and be open to invest time, money, and effort.

A Resilient Organisation cannot be built with herd mentality or playing it safe. It needs to constantly challenge the status quo. And not be fettered by analysis paralysis. It has to take calculated risk and manage it. It has to keep exploring better options, discover alternatives and tread new pathways. It has to perennially aspire, evolve, innovate, accelerate and scale. Innovation in product, process, marketing, organization….

Develop an ecosystem to drive value creation. Not just build on past, but also reinvent. Future-proof the organisation and turn threats into opportunities. Renew, adapt and change or risk becoming obsolete.

As the world faces multiple crises (including the existential crisis of climate change) and as we hurtle towards global uncertainty and geopolitical risk, the need for Organisational Resilience has increased manifold. A vision limited to the next quarter will not work. The author dwells on the McKinsey Global Institute study which concluded "that those with a long-term view outperformed the rest in earnings, revenue, investment, and job growth. Also, that companies with strong environmental, social, and governance (ESG) norms recorded higher performance and credit ratings; such companies perform better during crises." Long-term sustainability program needs to be aligned with business.

Truly, people make Resilient Organisations. Companies need to be employee-centric, respect and value their people and leverage the creativity of their own people. Develop empathy and trust. Build, maintain, and enhance relationships. "Take care of your people and people will take care of your business."

The author quotes Steve Jobs: "My job is to take these great people we have and to push them and make them even better."

Leaders need to walk the talk. Lead by example. By ethical principles.

To build the workforce of the future, Sood suggests mindset shifts, proactive upskilling and reskilling based on strategy needs and industry trends, building a scalable learning infrastructure, investing in a learning culture. To drive transformation, have a Chief Change Officer "whose cross-functional role is dedicated to helping prepare for a change-heavy future." Make innovation everyone's job, make transformation everyone's goal, make reinvention everyone's priority.

Be transparent and nurture optimism. Believe in the power of possibility. Prepare for the worst case.

Manage for truth and realism. Practice accountability. Collaborate and succeed together.

The author's 5-point mantra for personal resilience:

- To be strong physically
- To be strong mentally
- To be strong intellectually
- To be strong spiritually
- To be strong financially

It would be great interest to explore Daman's Thermometer – which sieves the facts from rumours and demonstrates resilient behaviour. Curious to see Daman's case studies on this.

Miracles may happen. But this small book can ensure that miracles happen. Miracles in Organisational Resilience.

Highly recommended for all.

2.5 Prof. K Subramanian

IEEE Ambassador, EX- SR. DDG(NIC), Min of C & IT & IT Adviser to CAG of India.

It is very inspiring to read the book written by shri Daman Dev Sood, flow of writing, in a story telling mode and emphasis on the topic chosen with good examples and lucid descriptions. This clearly shows the author's deep practical knowledge on the subject and has wide industry experience and implementation and training the trainers and leaders to understand the importance of Business Resilience than BCP & DR. His capacity building experience is clearly visible in the flow of writing and citation by examples.

This book is well organised, and chapters and contents reflect the knowledge of the author and his wide experience in various sectors of industry and government, and his writing and presentation skills.

He did mention that there would be less of what is so obvious (e.g. Business Continuity Management, Crisis Management, Risk Management, IT Disaster Recovery, Information/ Cyber Security etc.) and lot more of the not so obvious portions of the Organisational Resilience e.g. People, Board, Relationships, Creativity, Innovation, Empowerment, Procurement, Finance, Strategy etc. and I found the book to be full of such examples, stories, and chapters. He has not left anything uncovered.

Daman in his own style emphasises the following:

- Encourages to think out of the box;
- Encourages to do differently;
- Advocates to create a culture of speaking up, expressing fearlessly one's views;
- Expects to create a culture of listening to others' point of view;
- Demands to be open to invest (time, money, and effort)

These qualities emphasise good leadership → leads to Good Governance and organisational/national resilience in good and bad times.

He goes beyond Steve Jobs and states that to be resilient just recruiting the best is not enough – that needs to be followed by equally effective induction, engagement, and retention.

His quote: "extract best - focus on strengths and get the best, rather than attempting to fix the weaknesses: This is well emphasised in his book. This is the way of recruiting, training and retention of future workforce talent acquisition, development, and retention.

Daman ensembled 10 leadership qualities, leaving space for the reader to add many more. In the same chapter, he has defined the Balanced Score Card concept in his simple words – taking care of seemingly diverse forces" - finance, employees, customer, internal processes" is resilience.

Daman clearly distinguishes between some relationship between the ISO 22301 (BCM) and ISO 22316 (Organisational Resilience). He clearly explains the difference between the two and argues that sustainability needs Organization resilience than BCM.

He clearly details out VMV (with multiple examples) and emphasises the importance of purpose and how to achieve excellence. He quotes from McKinsey's, HBR and others extensively to emphasise the purpose and how to achieve excellence keeping VMVs in focus.

Curiosity, Initiative, Opportunity, Innovation, and positive thinking and utilising the opportunities is way to grow for sustenance. This is the new mantra.

I recommend this book to all, beginners to experts to read and practise to achieve excellence in whatever they do personally, institutionally, nationally/Globally.

This will lead to resilience.

2.6 Praveen Jain

Dy. Gen. Manager (L&PA), GAIL (India) Ltd., Noida

Going through the book *My Experiments with Organisational Resilience* is exciting and enriching reading experience. Daman has exquisitely shared his long journey of experiences on Organisational Resilience. He has attempted to give a deep dive into the subject, which has much broader scope than the Business Continuity Management. He has touched upon various important facets on Organisational Resilience through easy and interesting stories and references. Reader will surely embrace the book and contemplate – What next?

The author has emphasised that Risk Managing, Learning and Continually Improving Organisation is a Resilient Organisation. The book has become more relevant in the post-covid turmoil and the ongoing global challenges and uncertainties across the industry. Organisations are constantly challenged for survival in the dynamic environment and face uphill task at every moment. The learnings and experiences shared in the book are handy references and are advance and timely rescuer – both from internal and external threats.

The book is a valued collection of Organisational Resilience notions, which are vital and are easy to comprehend. The concepts are equally applicable both at macro level for the Organisations and at micro level for each individual where one can correlate and mitigate probable threats and their likely impacts.

The saying *Gagar me Sagar is* apt for this book and the learnings shall surely alleviate the thinking process and contribute to find the well-timed and treasured solutions for the endurance of the Organisations globally.

‘ The book is surely recommended for all personal / official libraries.’

2.7 Siddharth Sorout

CISSP

Its an amazing book written by an SME with decades of experience.

Why should you read it?

a) It will help you to become an effective leader who can drive the change.

b) Make your organization, team, and You to make resilience in all walks of life.

c) Every page brings lots of information and covering research papers which difficult to find in our busy schedule.

Happy Reading!

2.8 San

 San

Resilience is beyond BCM

Reviewed in India on 19 December 2022

Most see resilience as how soon you can get back to normal when disaster hits, but resilience is beyond that as explained in this book. This is a collection of experiences penned by Daman with no technical jargon, applicable to all organizations, and individuals can refer to this to become good leader. We are a startup and I look forward to practicing this in our own organization.

Helpful Report abuse

2.9 PG

 PG

★★★★★ **Practical Personal Professional (3P) approach covered in the book**

Reviewed in India on 5 December 2022

I loved the personal touch of the book. It also gives very useful advice on practical parts of life - how we need resilience not only in professional life but also in every aspect of our personal life.

Highly recommended.

Daman is an award-winning author, and now I can see why. His multi-decade experience is so well reflected in this book.

One person found this helpful

2.10 Ratna Pawan

Ratna Pawan

Interesting narration, thereby making the reading both informative and enjoyab

Reviewed in India on 22 November 2022

Daman is not only an experienced award winning risk professional but has a very interesting way c
conveying his ideas and thoughts. Great read here

One person found this helpful

Helpful | Report abuse

2.11 M L Kabir

Preamble: As I start drawing on the finishing touches to this post on reviewing the book by Daman Dev Sood on Organizational Resilience, I see a Gmail notification flashing on my laptop screen from McKinsey Data Points requesting me to join one of their surveys on Organizational Resilience. I consider myself lucky to have finished reading the book by Daman Dev Sood before that and it gives me the confidence now to do justice to the survey which starts with the first para heading titled 'Resilience Matters'.

It would not be out of context here to admit that my interest in organizational sustainability has had a natural trigger for being involved and led a number of sustainability initiatives of my employer at the later part of work life in the organization and also my curiosity into the aspect that what made my organization sailing and thriving through its more than 175 years of existence. This interest has gone on increasing in the last couple of years through the posts and communication by Daman Dev Sood on LinkedIn through which I have remained connected and updated on this all-important subject of Organizational Resilience.

The Book & the Author: I procured this book (on Amazon) "My Experiments With Truth Organizational Resilience – Part I" about a month back and finished reading the same now about a week ago. A less than 100 pages book quantitatively would have taken a lesser time to read but for the reason it takes longer are its quality contents which makes you travel down memory lane and relate many incident from our work life to the host of snippets that Daman Dev Sood illustrates in his unique style of 'no mincing of words' since he lives by his commitment doing justice to the title.

The book is uniquely structured with first 15 pages devoted to making the reader acquainted with the concept of Organizational Resilience since many like me would have otherwise faced the challenge of understanding the relatively lesser-known domain of Organizational Resilience. In the next couple of sections I would make the readers aware of my various learnings and takes after reading the book. I have bifurcated the book in two sections for easier presentations of my learnings before the readers and they are as Section – 1 comprising of 4 chapters (Chapter 1 to 4) that deal with understanding the concept of Organizational Resilience as envisioned by the author and Sec – 2 deals with a few selected snippets from a long list of 69 of them each one conveying a clear message of various aspects of resilience in an organizational context. The ones touched upon by me are my so-called favorite ones which I have understood and could relate to my own experience in corporate life. Organizational Resilience is a vast subject and rapidly evolving. In the words of the author himself "I guess it will take a decade at least to be comfortable with the subject – only if one starts practicing now."

My review is not from the angle of an expert on the subject since I am still a learner and wish to enjoy this learning journey to its fullest in not only benefitting myself but also for the benefits of all others. I am deeply touched by the humility of the author who has had deep exposure to the subject of Organizational Resilience for nearly 20 years and known to be an authority in India and abroad, when he says "Come, walk with me on this journey of 'learning and sharing forever'" and I also resonate these feelings as a baby learner of this subject.

Sec -1

There are 4 chapters here from Chapter 1 to Chapter 4 which deals with the fundamental aspects of the subject of Organizational Resilience. Here the author connects the reader to the core of the subject by differentiating it from BCM or other areas of Crisis or Risk Management of an enterprise. The focus is here on the VMV (Vision, Mission and Value) approach. He has taken a real life organizational mission statement of an enterprise and points out which element can make a difference to make the organization a resilient one. The reference to the ISO 22316:2017 is very relevant in this regard on the basis of which the author designed the 20 Block Monster Truck Model which could be termed as an exhaustive structure of a resilient organization.

The leadership role is well illustrated in Chapter – 3 where it is beautifully emphasized that mere recording lessons does not help but learning and sharing such learning with the external world makes it a leading organization. He says that risk managing, learning and continually improving organization with a balanced approach make the organization truly resilient. This section also touches upon the concept of 'balanced approach' and illustrates with an example from his own and concludes with the statement 'The first steppingstone in Organizational Resilience is the Great Leadership'.

Chapter – 4 describes the result of a LinkedIn poll conducted by the author to evaluate and assess whether Covid-19 pandemic made the BCM – Organizational Resilience more valued or not and I leave it for the readers to go through the same when they read this book.

Sec -2

Under the snippets which are divided into 69 sub-sections under Chapter – 5, I would like to touch upon the topics that have appeared more familiar and appealing to me thru' my humble exposure to the subject of organizational sustainability. They are coincidentally 10 in number, and I categorize them as Top 10 in my understanding of Organizational Resilience. However, this selection has nothing to do with the importance and impact of the other 59 topics covered by Sri Daman Dev Sood in his unique style with all having their own relevance and connect with Organizational Resilience.

Topic Sl No. 5.5 Creativity – I always wondered that an organization to be surviving the taste of time must be creative – it may not demonstrate the same externally but surely it would be a creative one internally. The creativity diagram I Picture 8 appears to me very exhaustive and surely the organization need to embrace them all in varying degrees to be resilient and successful over a time horizon.

Topic Sl No. 5.6 to 5.8 VMV – Readers would be greatly benefitted through the understanding of the 3 VMV modules explained in these chapters. The VMV 2 is exceptionally well designed thru' linkages of ISO modules on BCM and Resilience and I personally love the point on culture that differentiates the two ISO modules. The concept of shared vision, mission and values are the foundations of collaboration and co-creation in today's fast changing technology environment driven by digitalization.

Topic Sl No. 5.16 People Resilience – "Atom makes molecules and molecules make matter – Humane make organizations which all that matter" – an old saying still so true. The author mentions it more than once in the book that 'Resilient people make resilient organization'. It is people resilience that hold a team together and finally hold the organization together in its journey thru' challenging phases of its life cycles. Also suggest read Topic Sl No. 5.52 Respect and be Resilient & Topic Sl No. 5.59 Retain Employees and Be Resilient in the matter of People Resilience.

Topic Sl No. 5.40 Organizational Resilience & Sustainibility – The author attempts to relate organizational resilience and its close linkages to the UNSDGs which is interesting. Our country has committed to the UNSDGs timeline, and it is so very relevant that organizational resilience has to factor such aspects into its list of actions to remain resilient. I would also suggest that the readers go through Topic Sl No. 5.22 to 5.29 which deals with ESG and EHS topics in relation to organizational resilience which would be a full circle in this regard to remain sustainable.

Topic Sl No. 5.64 Simplify and Win – The organization with a purpose would be a resilient one. This chapter picks up a very important topic of connecting and redefining the purpose and that too during the crisis time. The tips provided are absolutely apt and relevant under any given situation.

Conclusion – At the end the book makes an enjoyable reading and dispels any fear on learning and mastering a vast subject like Organizational Resilience. The great deal of simplicity with which various concepts are explained with many a real life examples in each chapter and this simplicity runs thru' as a common thread in this book – I believe that this simple approach is expected to trigger fire to curiosity & inquisitiveness in reader's mind to go more in depth into the subject of Resilience.

The other aspect of the book which appeals most is that the author has made Organizational Resilience as a common man's subject thereby breaking the general myth of it being the sole monopoly and domain of extraordinarily intelligent and top bracket people. In a country like ours where even enterprises in the organized sectors shy away from the topic and the academic curriculum of institutes would have just started to include this in their curriculum, launching a book on Organizational Resilience in this backdrop aiming to reach one and all is certainly a very bold move by the author.

We look forward to seeing more such work from the author in future.

Wishing all readers, a very happy reading.

2.12 Mark Carroll

SVP – Business Risk Officer, Income Research + Management

"Interesting read. A lot there covering a ton of ground.".

A lot here so a bit of a challenge to provide explicit commentary.

That said, a few things stick out for me:

Leadership – the fact that management needs to lead by example and that management behavior cascades through the organization, good or bad. This is a tricky dynamic in that management needs to value its own time, and as a result delegate lesser tasks, but at the same time make sure that the troops recognize a willingness to engage in details as necessary. A few stories come to mind:

A large, global firm that was struggling with revenues and stock price dropping significantly over time, yet with

70% of the workforce 'Exceeding Expectations.' CEO stated that with the firm struggling and his office NOT meeting expectations in his eyes and that of the public, how could this level of performance at the employee level be even close to reasonable? He re-baselined performance in the firm to reflect a direct connection between his office and that of the detailed organization;

That of the CEO of a $120MM corporation (back in the 1980's when that was somewhat sizeable) going through engineering drawings in a board room because they could not get agreement on round head vs. pan head screws in equipment. The CEO shows willingness to get engaged but very little leadership operating in that capacity;

The billionaire CEO of a major financial services firm at a firm party in restroom where stall door would not shut. Another woman offered to 'guard the door'. Afterwards that CEO said, 'now your turn, I will watch the door.' That story rippled through the firm to the CEO's merit.

It shows great acumen and devotion to take on tasks that are needed that fall into the 'white space' and a leader who performs those tasks should be applauded. I use a BCDR crisis as a example, where risk/recovery planning takes a back seat to immediate needs – the BCDR team activities are NOT a critical function at-time-of and the team often winds up 'carrying water' for someone else. Too much of that confuses employees as to the role of BCDR and gets the team labeled as 'Gunga Din'.

Machiavelli would disagree with the direct mapping of a 'good guy' to leadership. I would agree that the trait is important, but ultimately the leader needs to consider 'the greatest good for the greatest number.' That could translate into a lay off of (say) 5% of the firm to ensure jobs for the other 95%. The 5% don't see a 'good guy' either because they don't have visibility into the firm-level risk OR they do and don't understand 'why me?' History is riddled with bloated firms that failed due to a cost structure that did not address the bloat.

Separately, for junior or inexperienced employees, what are the options for emulating or learning from senior leaders? Junior employees need that constant interaction with managers and fellow employees so learn 'what to do' and, just as valuable, 'what NOT to do', but are being denied that exposure. Email correspondence and light hybrid interaction just won't do it, especially for those in the early days of their 'career lifecycle.'

I like the 6 dimension of resilience as long as the focus within the 6 varies by organizational maturity. For example, a newly formed small business cares much more about operational issues such as liquidity than does a more established business. Conversely, the startup is not even thinking about brand and reputation but rather survival. Should the new firm fail, they will simply set up shop up the road with a new name since they really have no intangible brand value at this point. That scale will tip over time as their reputation is built and their brand develops its own value.

DEI and the Great Resignation is interesting in that firms are focused on their DEI numbers but have no real way to affect the demographic of those leaving. For example, if 75% of the resigning folks are women, minorities, etc. then the DEI metrics degrade considerably and not because of a lack of DEI attention. On a related note, it seems to me that the DEI focus is D and not E or I. For example, while Head of DEI certainly knows the D breakdown, does that person have any insight into compensation? Doubtful and without that, E takes a back seat to D.

Resilience as a term has no meaning without context, partially because it means something different to all parties. I compare this to the BCDR world where Hot and Cold sites are pretty well understood, but Warm site has no meaning without clarification since it is on a continuum between hot and cold. Where on that continuum is the result of further inquiry. Following that logic, Resilience or Operational Resilience is an analog or degree status rather than a digital binary status.

Section 3: Bonus Chapters

3.1 ABC's of Risk Management

Included here with permission from the owners of the document.

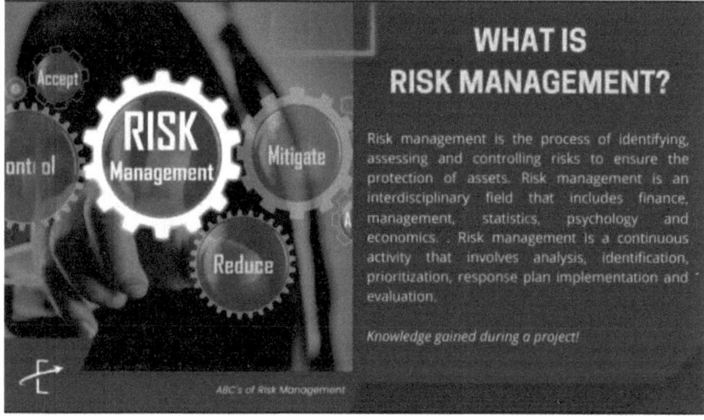

avoid risk
A
IS FOR
AVOIDANCE
Risk avoidance involves eliminating or avoiding a particular risk altogether. This may involve avoiding certain activities or situations that pose a risk to the organization, or choosing alternative strategies or solutions that do not involve the risk.
ABC's of Risk Management

B
IS FOR
BLACK SWAN
A black swan event is a rare and unpredictable event with severe consequences, such as a natural disaster, economic collapse, or major technological disruption. Black swan events can have a significant impact on an organization's operations, finances, and reputation, and effective risk management strategies should take into account the possibility of such events occurring.
ABC's of Risk Management

Control
C IS FOR CONTROL
Control refers to the process of implementing measures to manage or mitigate risks. Control measures can include policies, procedures, technology solutions, and other strategies to reduce the likelihood and/or impact of identified risks. Effective risk management requires the implementation of appropriate controls to manage and mitigate risks.
ABC's of Risk Management

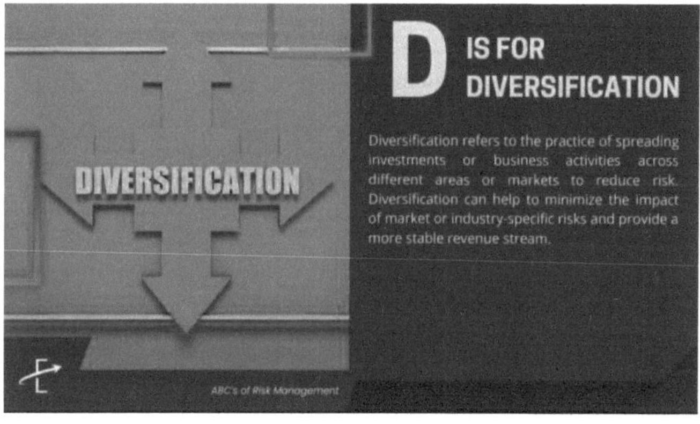
DIVERSIFICATION
D IS FOR DIVERSIFICATION
Diversification refers to the practice of spreading investments or business activities across different areas or markets to reduce risk. Diversification can help to minimize the impact of market or industry-specific risks and provide a more stable revenue stream.
ABC's of Risk Management

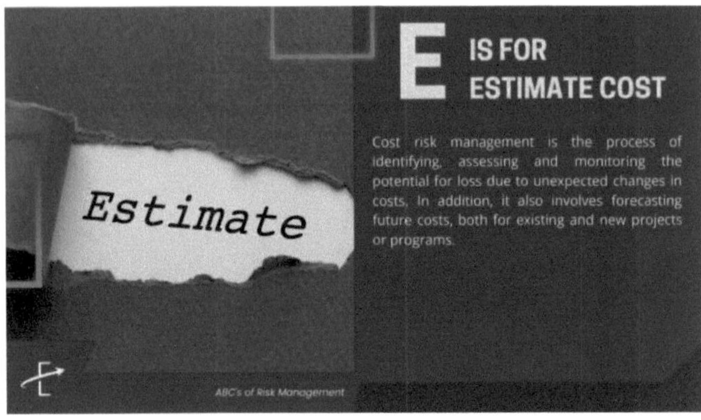
Estimate
E IS FOR ESTIMATE COST
Cost risk management is the process of identifying, assessing and monitoring the potential for loss due to unexpected changes in costs. In addition, it also involves forecasting future costs, both for existing and new projects or programs.
ABC's of Risk Management

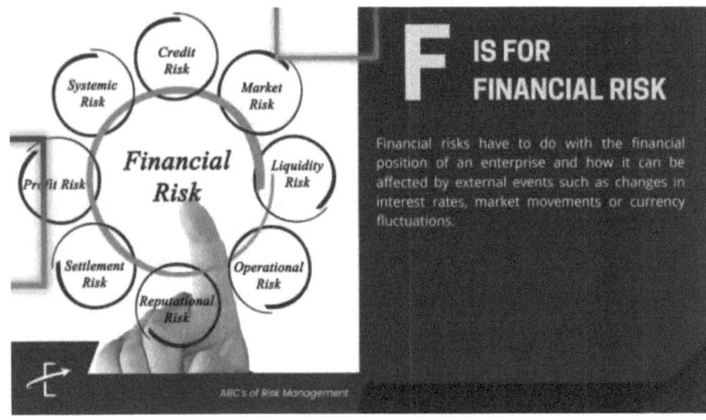
Credit Risk
Systemic Risk
Market Risk
Financial Risk
Profit Risk
Liquidity Risk
Settlement Risk
Operational Risk
Reputational Risk
F IS FOR FINANCIAL RISK
Financial risks have to do with the financial position of an enterprise and how it can be affected by external events such as changes in interest rates, market movements or currency fluctuations.
ABC's of Risk Management

G IS FOR GEOPOLITICAL RISK
Geopolitical risk refers to the risk of economic, political, or social instability in a particular country or region. Geopolitical risks can include factors such as political unrest, terrorism, war, and changes in government policies or regulations.
ABC's of Risk Management

H IS FOR HAZARD
A hazard is a potential source of harm or danger that can cause injury, damage to property, or other negative consequences. Hazard identification is a critical part of the risk management process, as it helps organizations to identify potential sources of risk and implement appropriate controls to manage them.
ABC's of Risk Management

INSURANCE
I IS FOR INSURANCE
Insurance is a risk management tool that involves transferring the financial risk of a potential loss to an insurance company. Effective insurance risk management involves identifying potential risks, selecting appropriate insurance coverage, and regularly reviewing and updating insurance policies.
ABC's of Risk Management

955 Jurisdiction
J IS FOR JURISDICTIONAL RISK
Jurisdictional risk refers to the potential risks associated with doing business in a particular geographic location or jurisdiction, such as a country or region with a less stable political or legal system. Effective jurisdictional risk management involves identifying potential risks, conducting thorough due diligence, and implementing appropriate risk management strategies, such as diversifying operations across multiple jurisdictions or developing contingency plans for potential disruptions.
ABC's of Risk Management

KPI
K IS FOR KPI
Having reliable metrics or key performance indicators (KPIs) in the field of information security is a prerequisite to building a successful security program. Measuring operational efficiency, costs and benefits has always been a concern for managers, and information security is no exception.
ABC's of Risk Management

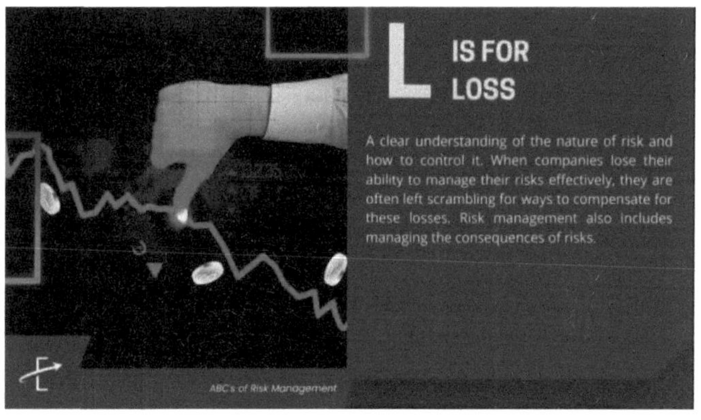
L IS FOR LOSS
A clear understanding of the nature of risk and how to control it. When companies lose their ability to manage their risks effectively, they are often left scrambling for ways to compensate for these losses. Risk management also includes managing the consequences of risks.
ABC's of Risk Management

M IS FOR MITIGATION
Mitigation refers to the process of implementing measures to reduce the likelihood and/or impact of identified risks. Mitigation measures can include policies, procedures, technology solutions, and other strategies to reduce the potential impact of identified risks.
Risk Mitigation
ABC's of Risk Management

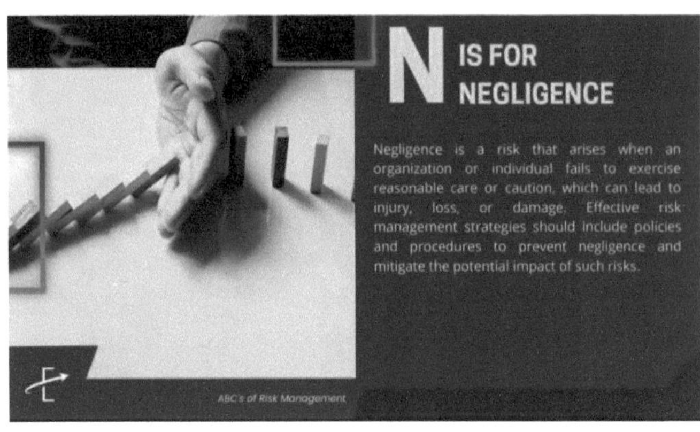
N IS FOR NEGLIGENCE
Negligence is a risk that arises when an organization or individual fails to exercise reasonable care or caution, which can lead to injury, loss, or damage. Effective risk management strategies should include policies and procedures to prevent negligence and mitigate the potential impact of such risks.
ABC's of Risk Management

O
IS FOR
OPPORTUNITY
COST
Opportunity cost refers to the potential cost of foregone opportunities, such as choosing one investment opportunity over another. Effective opportunity cost management involves identifying potential risks and opportunities, analyzing trade-offs, and making informed decisions that maximize potential benefits and minimize potential costs.
ABC's of Risk Management

product liability
P
IS FOR
PRODUCT
LIABILITY
Product liability refers to the potential legal and financial risks associated with the manufacture and sale of products, such as defects, recalls, or lawsuits. Effective product liability risk management involves implementing appropriate quality control measures, conducting thorough testing and validation, and providing clear instructions and warnings to customers.
ABC's of Risk Management

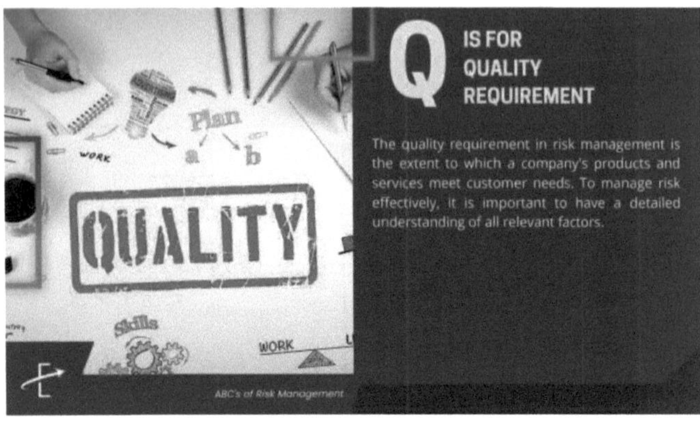
Plan
a
b
WORK
QUALITY
Skills
WORK
Q IS FOR QUALITY REQUIREMENT
The quality requirement in risk management is the extent to which a company's products and services meet customer needs. To manage risk effectively, it is important to have a detailed understanding of all relevant factors.
ABC's of Risk Management

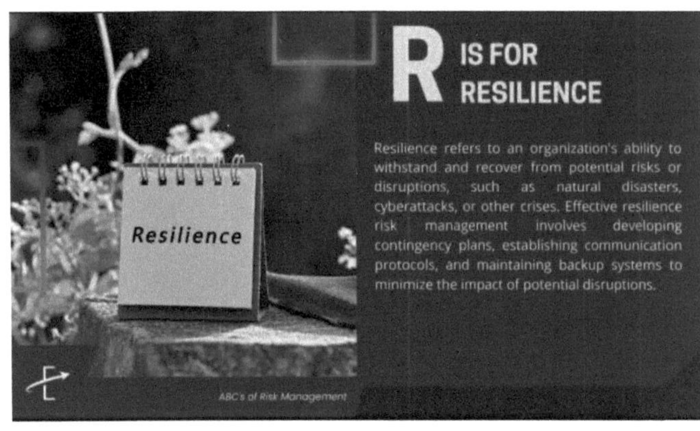
R IS FOR RESILIENCE
Resilience
Resilience refers to an organization's ability to withstand and recover from potential risks or disruptions, such as natural disasters, cyberattacks, or other crises. Effective resilience risk management involves developing contingency plans, establishing communication protocols, and maintaining backup systems to minimize the impact of potential disruptions.
ABC's of Risk Management

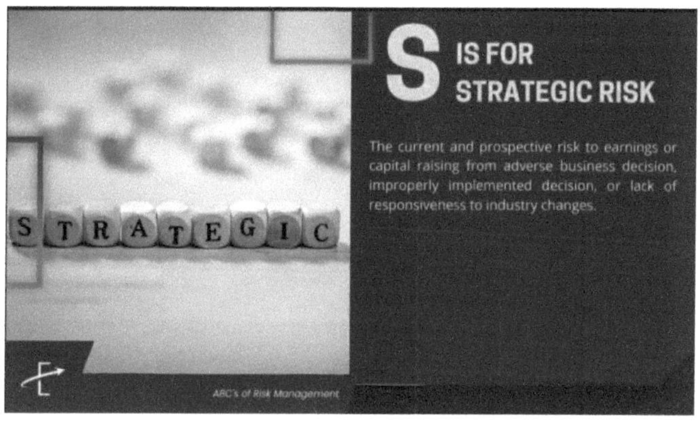
S IS FOR
STRATEGIC RISK
The current and prospective risk to earnings or capital raising from adverse business decision, improperly implemented decision, or lack of responsiveness to industry changes.
STRATEGIC
ABC's of Risk Management

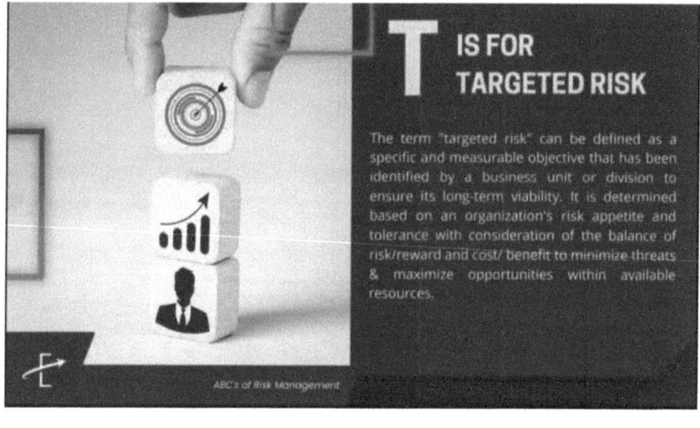
T IS FOR
TARGETED RISK
The term "targeted risk" can be defined as a specific and measurable objective that has been identified by a business unit or division to ensure its long-term viability. It is determined based on an organization's risk appetite and tolerance with consideration of the balance of risk/reward and cost/ benefit to minimize threats & maximize opportunities within available resources.
ABC's of Risk Management

U IS FOR UNCERTAINTY
Uncertainty refers to the potential risk of financial loss associated with unpredictable or unknown events, such as changes in market conditions or unexpected disruptions. Effective uncertainty risk management involves identifying potential risks, developing contingency plans, and regularly monitoring and reviewing market conditions to mitigate the impact of potential uncertainties.
ABC's of Risk Management

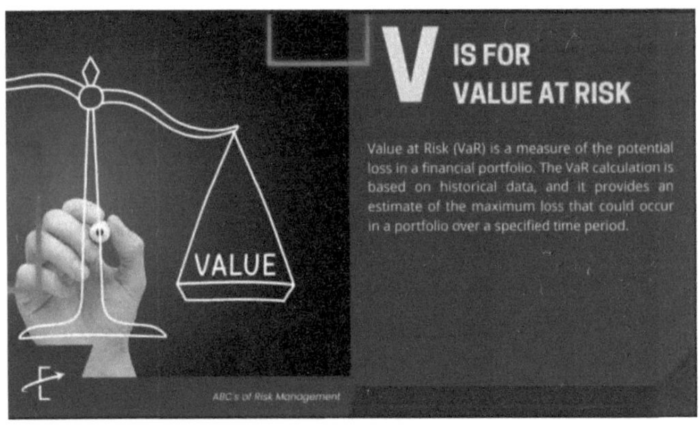
V IS FOR VALUE AT RISK
Value at Risk (VaR) is a measure of the potential loss in a financial portfolio. The VaR calculation is based on historical data, and it provides an estimate of the maximum loss that could occur in a portfolio over a specified time period.
VALUE
ABC's of Risk Management

W
IS FOR
WEALTH
PRESERVATION
Wealth preservation refers to the process of protecting and preserving an individual's or organization's financial assets. Effective wealth preservation risk management involves identifying potential risks, implementing appropriate risk management strategies, and regularly monitoring and adjusting investment strategies to manage potential risks.
ABC's of Risk Management

EXPECT
RESULT
X
IS FOR
EXPECTED VALUE
Expected value can be calculated for any type of financial asset e.g., stocks, bonds, and options. Expected value has two (2) components; the probability of distribution of possible outcomes, and the mean or average outcome.
ABC's of Risk Management

Y IS FOR
YIELD RISK
Yield risk refers to the potential risk of financial loss associated with changes in the yield or return of an investment, such as a bond or stock. Effective yield risk management involves identifying potential risks, diversifying investments, and regularly monitoring and adjusting investment strategies to manage the impact of changes in yield or return."
ABC's of Risk Management

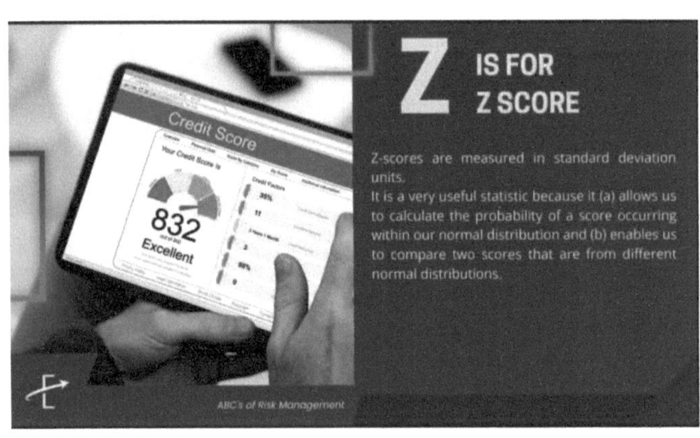
Z IS FOR
Z SCORE
Z-scores are measured in standard deviation units.
It is a very useful statistic because it (a) allows us to calculate the probability of a score occurring within our normal distribution and (b) enables us to compare two scores that are from different normal distributions.
Credit Score
832
Excellent
ABC's of Risk Management

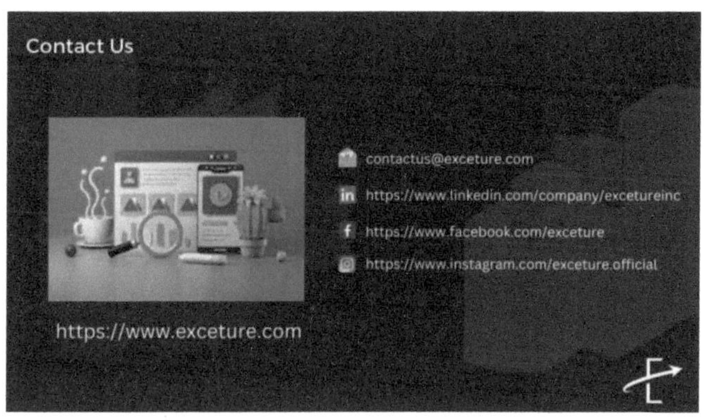
Contact Us
contactus@exceture.com
https://www.linkedin.com/company/excetureinc
https://www.facebook.com/exceture
https://www.instagram.com/exceture.official
https://www.exceture.com

3.2 Let your employees 'SLEEP'

Rashmi Keshwani

Head B2B Training - Indian Leadership Academy l ICF Certified Communication Coach l Soft skills Trainer l Key note Speaker l L&D Lead l Certified Zumba Fitness Instructor

Yes, u heard that right!!! 😀

Before this sparks any debates, let Me share that when an employee is not well rested or his/her wellbeing not given due importance, it can

👉Hamper their productivity

👉Impair their safety awareness leading to work related injuries or ailments

👉 Lead to low morale

👉 Reduce creative abilities

👉 Result in higher Employee turnover

All this due to a Cognitive overload, resulting in a Burnout like feeling, anxiety, stress and constant sense of not having completed something.

Well in my slightly satirical but sincere attempt, here's how u can ensure ur Employees SLEEP, maybe not literally.

It's time organisations must ensure that there is enough priority given to creating an environment that helps reduce stress and promotes ones well being.

S – Structure

Sharing a structure and providing clarity in one's role can help individuals contribute to better decision making leading to increased productivity. Not having clarity can lead to chaos and frustration and subsequently stressful work environment.

L – Learning

Encouraging learning through Self learning, training/coaching can help employees develop skills & knowledge, acquire abilities making them more proficient and making them feel more cared for.

🔈E – Engage

Engage with employess at a human level!!! Not only will it keep them aligned to the organisational goals, but also will win their trust and loyalty.

🔈E – Endorse

It is absolutely essential to Endorse one's skills, recognize and reward whenever and wherever appropriate.. This is guaranteed to motivate them and inspire teams around them. Making one feel more valued, thus building strong and successful teams...

🔈P - and lastly the essence of SLEEP, NO NOT performance or productivity or positivity, is all about that POWER NAP or a reasonable Break in between tasks through the day.. An effective way to Reset and Refocus on a challenging day..

So, For the sake of the WELL BEING of the organisation and its employees, Embrace S.L.E.E.P 🙏 😊

In my own words

In football, power is not how big a muscle you have – its more about how less scared you are – Sunil Chhetri, Captain Indian Football Team.

This is a great example of personal resilience. Same is true about businesses also – risk taking is mandatory, not blindly though. Hence Risk Management is a key pillar in Resilience (Operational/ Organisational).

In the book, I say 'Risk Managing, Learning, and Continually Improving Organisation is a Resilient Organisation'.

Read my book 'My Experiments with Oganisational Resilience: Part-I' for as many as 69 snippets of this type that will help you to sell Organisational Resilience internally. You will also see that Organisational Resilience is much more than Business Continuity Management, Risk Management, Crisis Management, IT Disaster Recovery, Information and Cyber Security Management etc. You will see more of people angle in the book than the traditional beliefs of Resilience.

I invite you all to walk on this journey of 'learning & sharing' with me.

Reader's Views on Various Chapters

Daman Dev Sood, FBCI, FBCS, CBCI, SMIEEE, MAIMA, M.IOD, ISO 22301 LA & Expert

Certified in Cybersecurity (ISC2)

IEEE Ambassador

Past Chair – IEEE Computer Society Delhi Section Chapter

Chair – PR&P Standing Committee, IEEE Delhi Section

Member Champion – IEEE India MOVE Partner Relations Committee

IEEE Computer Society Distinguished Contributor (Inaugural Class)

Toastmaster

International Resilience Trainer & Consultant

Reskube Partner

Global Release - Global Emotional Impact Assessment Report – click here to download complimentary copy

Video profile: https://youtu.be/TuPmBmYDIms

Email: dbdsood@hotmail.com

Phone: +91 9958091880 (whatsapp)

https://www.damandevsood.com/

https://youtube.com/damandevsood

https://www.linkedin.com/in/damandevsood/

https://www.facebook.com/dbdsood

https://twitter.com/DamanDevSood

https://www.instagram.com/damandevsood/

https://medium.com/@damandevsood

https://in.pinterest.com/damandevsood

Author of "My Experiments with Organisational Resilience: Part-I" available at notionpress.com, amazon.in, flipkart.com

Author of "COPYRIGHT Cases – Resolved" available at notionpress.com, amazon.in, flipkart.com

Author of "My Experiments With BCM" available at notionpress.com, amazon.in, amazon.co.uk, amazon.com, flipkart.com, kriso.it, wob.com, barnesandnoble.com, ebook.de, books.google.co.in, fnac.com, bookdepository.com , shop.wordbookstores.com, fnac.pt, kiz zybooksandmore.com

Author of "Step by Step guide to the NCEMA 7000: Implement BCM the UAE way" - Available online at the Kindle store

DRI
2022
Lifetime Achievement Award
Finalist
DRI
2021
Lifetime Achievement Award
Finalist
RESKUBE
cc.
WINNER 2020
bci
Fellow
FELLOW
CERTIFICATE

My Courses

Key Features:

- 5 days
- 6 case studies
- 52 exercises
- 25 sample documents
- Modular approach
- No prerequisites
- 100 MCQ-120 minutes assessment

S. No.	Course	Duration	Standard/ Area	Type
1	Resiliency Testing	5 days	Resiliency	Instructor Led Online/ Classroom
2	Organisational Resilience Professional	1 day	ISO 22316:2017	Instructor Led Online/ Classroom
3	Organisational Resilience Specialist	3 days	ISO 22316:2017	Instructor Led Online/ Classroom
4	Risk Management Professional	1 day	ISO 31000:2018	Instructor Led Online/ Classroom
5	Risk Management Specialist	3 days	ISO 31000:2018	Instructor Led Online/ Classroom
6	Practical BIA (Specialist level)	2 days	BCM	Instructor Led Online/ Classroom

S. No.	Course	Duration	Standard/ Area	Type
7	Operational Resilience Foundation	½ day	Operational Resilience	Instructor Led Online/ Classroom
8	Operational Resilience Professional	1 day	Operational Resilience	Instructor Led Online/ Classroom
9	Design, Develop, and Deliver an Effective BCM Test	2 days	BCM	Instructor Led Online/ Classroom
10	Daman's Thermometer	1 day	Crisis Communication	Instructor Led Online/ Classroom
11	Possibility Thinking	1 day	Softskills	Instructor Led Online/ Classroom

S. No.	Course	Duration	Standard/ Area	Type
12	Team Work & Art of Handling Questions	1 day	Softskills	Instructor Led Online/ Classroom
13	Resiliency Testing (for top management)	2 days	Resiliency	Instructor Led Online/ Classroom
14	Cyber Resiliency Testing (for top management)	2 days	Resiliency	Instructor Led Online/ Classroom
15	Delivering Excellence	2 days	Resiliency	Instructor Led Online/ Classroom
16	Circular Economy, Life Cycle Analysis, ESG, and Sustainable Supply Chain	1 day	Sustainability	Instructor Led Online/ Classroom

Other Books

BUSINESS CONTINUITY
Implement BCM the UAE Way!
1st EDITION
STEP-BY-STEP GUIDE
AE/SCNS/NCEMA 7000:2015
Authors
DHIRAJ LAL
DAMAN DEV SOOD
TOWARDS NATIONAL RESILIENCE

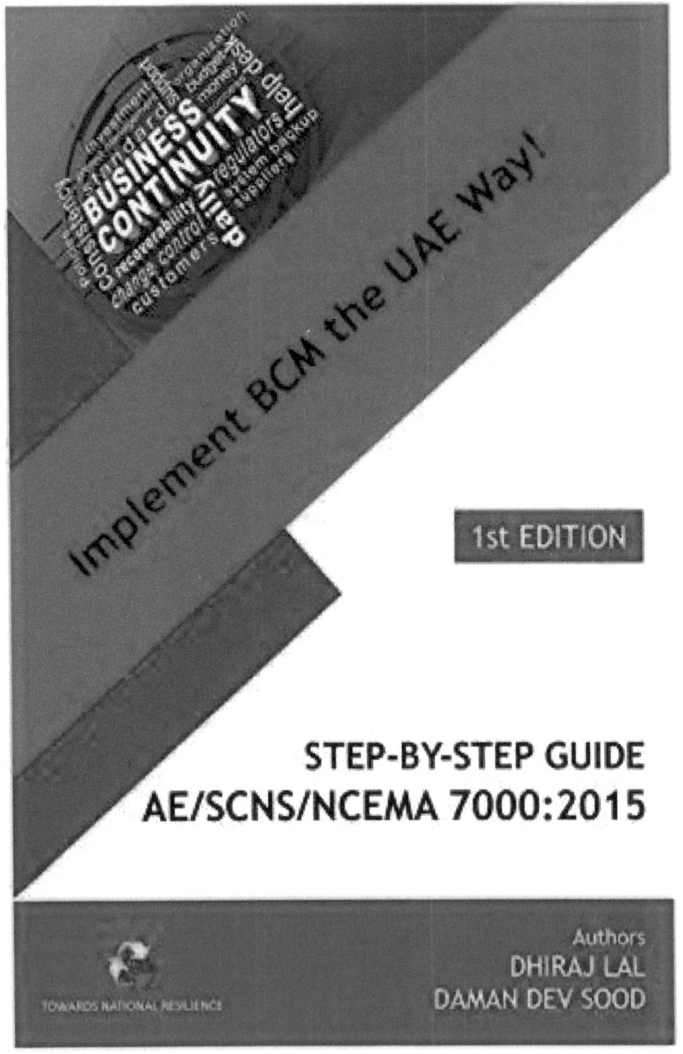

MY
EXPERIMENTS WITH
TRUTH BCM
MY BCM JOURNEY - YOUR BCM MENTOR/COMPANION
SUPPLY CHAIN CONTINUITY
DEPENDENCIES
BUDGET
IMPACT ANALYSIS
REVIEWS
RISK ASSESSMENT
INTERESTED PARTIES
CONTINUAL IMPROVEMENT
BUSINESS CONTINUITY MANAGEMENT
PLAN TESTING
CONTINUITY STRATEGIES
COMPETENCIES
REGULATORY REQUIREMENTS
CONTINUITY PLANS
IT DISASTER RECOVERY
DAMAN DEV SOOD

COPYRIGHT
Cases
Resolved

ANCHITA SOOD
DAMAN DEV SOOD
cover designed by- Tanuj Sood

My EXPERIMENTS with ~~TRUTH~~ ORGANISATIONAL RESILIENCE

Part-1

Financial control Management
Information Security Management
Fraud Control Management
Business Continuity Management
Human Resource Management
Strategic Planning Management
Crisis Management
Cyber Security Management
Health and Safety Management
ICT Management
Governance
Facilities Management
Emergency Management
Asset Management
Risk Management
Supply Chain Management
Communications Management
Environmental Management
Physical Security Management
Human Resource Management

DAMAN DEV SOOD

Printed by Libri Plureos GmbH in Hamburg,
Germany